# Nan Yar

## Who Am I?

Sri Ramana Maharshi

# Nan Yar

## Who Am I?

*The Essential Spiritual Teachings*

Translated from the original Tamil

# NAN YAR

Published by
Open Sky Press
Rheinstraße 56, 51371 Hitdorf
office@openskypress.com

All rights reserved. No part of this book may be used or
reproduced in any part whatsoever without written permission.
For further information please contact Open Sky Press.

Third Reprint 2023

© Open Sky Press 2015

ISBN 978-0-9574627-5-5

Photographs from Time Life / Getty Images by Eliot Elisofon: pp VI, 26
Photographs from Magnum Photo by Henri Cartier Bresson: pp 88, 91
Photographs from G. Boyd: pp 8, 20
All other photographs from Ramana Ashram.

Printed in Poland

**OPEN SKY PRESS**
**www.openskypress.com**

# Contents

Introduction . . . . . . . . . . . . . . . . . . . . . . . 1

Sri Ramana Maharshi
Biography . . . . . . . . . . . . . . . . . . . . . . . . . 5
Life Events . . . . . . . . . . . . . . . . . . . . . . . 6
About his Name . . . . . . . . . . . . . . . . . . . 7

Foreword Ken Wilber . . . . . . . . . . . . . . . 9

Who Am I? (Nan Yar) . . . . . . . . . . . . . 17

Glossary . . . . . . . . . . . . . . . . . . . . . . . . 93
Sri Ramana Book Selection . . . . . . . . . 98

# Who Am I?

When other thoughts arise, one should not pursue them, but should inquire: 'To whom do they arise?' It does not matter how many thoughts arise. As each thought arises, one should inquire with diligence, 'To whom has this thought arisen?' The answer that would emerge would be 'to me'.

Thereupon if one inquires 'Who am I?', the mind will go back to its source; and the thought that arose will become quiescent [*still*]. With repeated practice in this manner, the mind will develop the skill to stay in its source.

# Introduction

*Nan Yar*, meaning 'Who am I?', was originally spoken by Bhagavan Sri Ramana Maharshi in 1901, when he was twenty-one years old.

Following his spontaneous moment of realisation as a sixteen-year-old school boy, Sri Ramana was drawn to Arunachala, a holy mountain in South India, which he never left. It was while he was living in a cave on the mountain's slopes that he was questioned by a man called Sivaprakasam Pillai.

'Sri Ramana wrote his answers with his finger in the sand because this was the period in which he found it difficult to speak. Naturally this writing medium produced short, concise answers.

'Sivaprakasam Pillai didn't write down these answers. After each new question was asked, Sri Ramana wiped out his previous reply and wrote a new one in the sand. When he went home, Sivaprakasam Pillai wrote down what he could remember of this silent conversation.

'About twenty years later Sivaprakasam Pillai published these questions and answers as an appendix to a biography of Sri Ramana that he had written and published. There were thirteen questions and answers in this first published version.

'Sri Ramana's devotees appreciated this particular presentation. Ramana Ashram published it as a separate booklet, and with each edition more and more questions and answers were added. The longest version has about thirty.

'At some point in the 1920s Sri Ramana himself rewrote this series of questions and answers as a prose essay, elaborating on some answers and deleting others. This is now published under the title *Who Am I?* in Sri Ramana's *Collected Works* and separately as this small book. It is Sri Ramana's summary of answers written more than twenty years before.'\*

*Nan Yar*, or *Who Am I?* contains the core of Sri Ramana's teachings with a focus on Self-inquiry. Although Sri Ramana had not studied the scriptures when he first answered the questions, it is a spiritual classic that is in line with both the *Vedanta*\* [*Indian philosophy*] and *Yoga* traditions. He answered the questions posed to him that day from the Self\*, reflecting the ancient wisdom of India and the contemporary wisdom of his time.

There is no doubt that the importance Sri Ramana gave to Self-inquiry as the most direct route to Self-realisation has attracted enormous attention from serious Western seekers of Truth in the last years. Not only his teachings have attracted attention but also his exemplary lifestyle and the *sattvic*\* [*pure*] nature of his mind - which are visibly reflected in the architecture of his ashram.

The paragraph that begins his essay was not given out in response to a question. It was composed by Sri Ramana when he was rewriting the work in the 1920s. Many philosophical works begin with a statement about the nature of happiness and the means by which it can be attained or discovered. Sri Ramana has followed this tradition.

It is with great pleasure that Open Sky Press has decided to make this classic text available in new translations in several European languages, ably supported by a host of recently digitally re-mastered photographs for which we thank Mr. Sundaram, President of Sri Ramana Ashram. A number of Sri Ramana's more important teaching quotations have been included.

*John David 2015 Open Sky Press*

\* Arunachala Shiva *page 47, published by Open Sky Press*

# Bhagavan Sri Ramana Maharshi

The Sage of Arunachala, born in 1879, is one of the most famous and most recent of India's wealth of sages, saints and spiritual Masters.

As a young man of sixteen he had a spontaneous awakening. He left his home in Madurai and made his way to the holy mountain Arunachala at Tiruvannamalai. He lived for many years, alone and in silence, on and around the mountain, which he never left. In the 1920s the present ashram was constructed. Here he lived and taught until his death in 1950.

Many students and devotees of this *Maha Rishi* [*great saint*], who gained Self-realisation through him, passed on to their own students Sri Ramana Maharshi's practice of Self-inquiry, using the question, 'Who am I?'

# Sri Ramana Life Events

| | |
|---|---|
| 1879 Dec 30 | Born in Tamil Nadu, South India, as Venkataraman |
| 1896 July | Spiritual Awakening aged sixteen |
| 1896 Sept 1 | Arrived at Arunachala |
| 1898 | Moved to Gurumurtham |
| 1899 | Moved to Virupaksha Cave aged nineteen |
| 1901 | First recorded teaching *Who Am I?* aged twenty-one |
| 1906-07 | Recovered his speech |
| 1907 | Given the name Bhagavan Sri Ramana Maharshi |
| 1916 | Mother arrived to live at Virupaksha Cave |
| 1917 | Moved to Skanda Ashram aged thirty-seven |
| 1922 May | Mother died and later Sri Ramana moved down the hill |
| 1920s | Sri Ramana rewrote and published *Who Am I?* |
| 1920s | Simple bamboo ashram buildings constructed |
| 1927-1942 | Stone ashram buildings constructed |
| 1930s | Paul Brunton visited |

| | |
|---|---|
| 1940s | New granite Hall built in front of Mother's Shrine |
| 1949 | Cancer appeared on Sri Ramana's arm |
| 1949 | Moved very ill to live in Samadhi Room |
| 1950 April 14 | Sri Ramana passed away at 8.47pm |

## Bhagavan Sri Ramana Maharshi

| | |
|---|---|
| Bhagavan | Living God |
| Sri | Honorific meaning illustrious |
| Ramana | One who knows he is the Self |
| | One who revels in the heart of all |
| Maha | Great |
| Rishi | Wise One / Pure Awareness |

The illustrious Saint who dwells in the heart of all.

# Foreword
## Ken Wilber
### The Sage of the Century

That Nondual vision in the form of *Vedanta**, is the precious gift of India to the world, and it found its purest, most elegant, most brilliant expression in the simple sage of Arunachala, Sri Ramana Maharshi.

His realisation came to him fully formed – or perhaps we should say, fully formless – and therefore it needed no further growth. He simply speaks from and as the absolute, the Self, the purest Emptiness that is the goal and ground of the entire manifest world, and is not other to that world. Sri Ramana, echoing *Shankara** [*Indian sage*], used to say:

> **The world is illusory;**
> ***Brahman**** **alone is real;**
> ***Brahman*** **is the world.**

This profound realisation is what separates Sri Ramana's genuine enlightenment from today's pretenders – deep ecology, Gaia revivals, Goddess worship, ecopsychology, systems theory, web-of-life notions – none of which have grasped the first two lines, and therefore, contrary to their sweet pronouncements, do not really understand the third. It is for all of those who are only in love with the manifest world – from capitalists to socialists, from green polluters to green peacers, from egocentrics to ecocentrists – that Sri Ramana's message needs so desperately to be heard.

What and where is this Self? How do I abide as That? There is no doubt how Sri Ramana would answer those – and virtually all other – questions: Who wants to know? What in you, right now, is aware of this page? Who is the Knower that knows the world but cannot itself be known? Who is the Hearer that hears the birds but cannot itself be heard? Who is the Seer that sees the clouds but cannot itself be seen?

And so arises Self-inquiry, Sri Ramana's special gift to the world. I have feelings, but I am not those feelings. Who am I? I have thoughts, but I am not those thoughts. Who am I? I have desires, but I am not those desires. Who am I?

So you push back into the Source of your own awareness – what Sri Ramana often called the 'I-I', since it is aware of the normal I or ego. You push back into the Witness, the I-I, and you rest as That. I am not objects, not feelings, not desires, not thoughts.

But then people usually make a rather unfortunate mistake in this Self-inquiry. They think that if they rest in the Self, or Witness, they are going to see something, or feel something, something really amazing, special, spiritual. But you won't see anything. If you see something, that is just another object – another feeling, another thought, another sensation, another image. But those are all objects; those are what you are not.

No, as you rest in the Witness – realising I am not objects, I am not feelings, I am not thoughts – all you will notice is a sense of Freedom, a sense of Liberation, a sense of Release – release from the terrible constriction of identifying with these little finite objects, the little body and little mind and little ego, all of which are objects that can be seen, and thus are not the true Seer, the real Self, the pure Witness, which is what you really are.

So you won't see anything in particular. Whatever is arising is fine. Clouds float by in the sky, feelings float by in the body, thoughts float by in the mind – and you can effortlessly witness all of them. They all spontaneously arise in your own present, easy, effortless awareness. And this witnessing awareness is not itself anything specific you can see. It is just a vast, background sense of Freedom – or pure Emptiness – and in that pure Emptiness, which you are, the entire manifest world arises. You are that Freedom, Openness, Emptiness – and not any little finite thing that arises in it.

Resting in that empty, free, easy, effortless witnessing, notice that the clouds are arising in the vast space of your awareness. The clouds are arising within you – so much so you can taste the clouds, you are one with the clouds, it is as if they are on this side of your skin, they are so close. The sky and your awareness have become one, and all things in the sky are floating effortlessly through your own awareness. You can kiss the sun, swallow the mountain, they are that close. Zen says 'Swallow the Pacific Ocean in a single gulp,' and that's the easiest thing in the world when inside and outside are no longer two, when subject and object are nondual, when the looker and looked at are One Taste.

And so: The world is illusory, which means you are not any object at all — nothing that can be seen is ultimately real. You are *neti-neti*, not this, not that. And under no circumstances should you base your salvation on that which is finite, temporal, passing, illusory, suffering-enhancing and agony-inducing.

*Brahman*\* [*absolute reality*] alone is real, the Self (unqualifiable *Brahman-Atman*\*) alone is real — the pure Witness, the timeless Unborn, the formless Seer, the radical I-I, radiant Emptiness — is what is real and all that is real. It is your condition, your nature, your essence, your present and your future, your desire and your destiny, and yet it is always ever-present as pure Presence, the alone that is Alone.

*Brahman* is the world, Emptiness and Form are not-two. After you realise that the manifest world is illusory, and after you realise that *Brahman* alone is real, then you can see that the absolute and the relative are not-two or nondual, then you can see that *nirvana*\* and *samsara*\* are not-two, then you can realise that the Seer and everything seen are not-two, *Brahman* and the world are not-two — all of which really means, the sound of those birds singing! The entire world of Form exists nowhere but in your own present Formless Awareness: You can drink the Pacific in a single gulp, because the entire world literally exists in your pure Self, the ever-present great I-I.

Finally, and most important, Sri Ramana would remind us that the pure Self – and therefore the great Liberation – cannot be attained, any more than you can attain your feet or acquire your lungs. You are already aware of the sky, you already hear the sounds around you, you already witness this world. One hundred percent of the enlightened mind or pure Self is present right now – not ninety-nine percent, but one hundred percent.

As Sri Ramana constantly pointed out, if the Self (or knowledge of the Self) is something that comes into existence – if your realisation has a beginning in time – then that is merely another object, another passing, finite, temporal state. There is no reaching the Self – the Self is reading this page. There is no looking for the Self – it is looking out of your eyes right now. There is no attaining the Self – it is reading these words. You simply, absolutely, cannot attain that which you have never lost. And if you do attain something, Sri Ramana would say, that's very nice, but that's not the Self.

So, if I may suggest, as you read the following words from the world's greatest sage: If you think you don't understand Self or Spirit, then rest in that which doesn't understand, and just that is Spirit. If you think you don't quite 'get' the Self or Spirit, then rest in that which doesn't quite get it, and just that is Spirit. Thus, if you think you understand Spirit, that is Spirit. If you think you don't, that is Spirit. And so we can leave with Sri Ramana's greatest and most secret message: The enlightened mind is not hard to attain but impossible to avoid.

*Ken Wilber 1999*

# Nan Yar

Sri Ramana Maharshi

# *Notes for the Reader*

Ramana Maharshi's original text is printed here exactly as he edited it in the 1920s. Where there is a Sanskrit word in the text we have given its meaning, italicised in square brackets. A Glossary entry for a Sanskrit word is marked in the text by a star*. Where the original translated English is old fashioned a modern word is offered, italicised in square brackets. The curved brackets are from the original text. In the case of some answers, for example question 1, we offer a simple modern essence of the Indian terminology under the original in italicised square brackets. In these ways we intend this important text to be more available to the contemporary general reader.

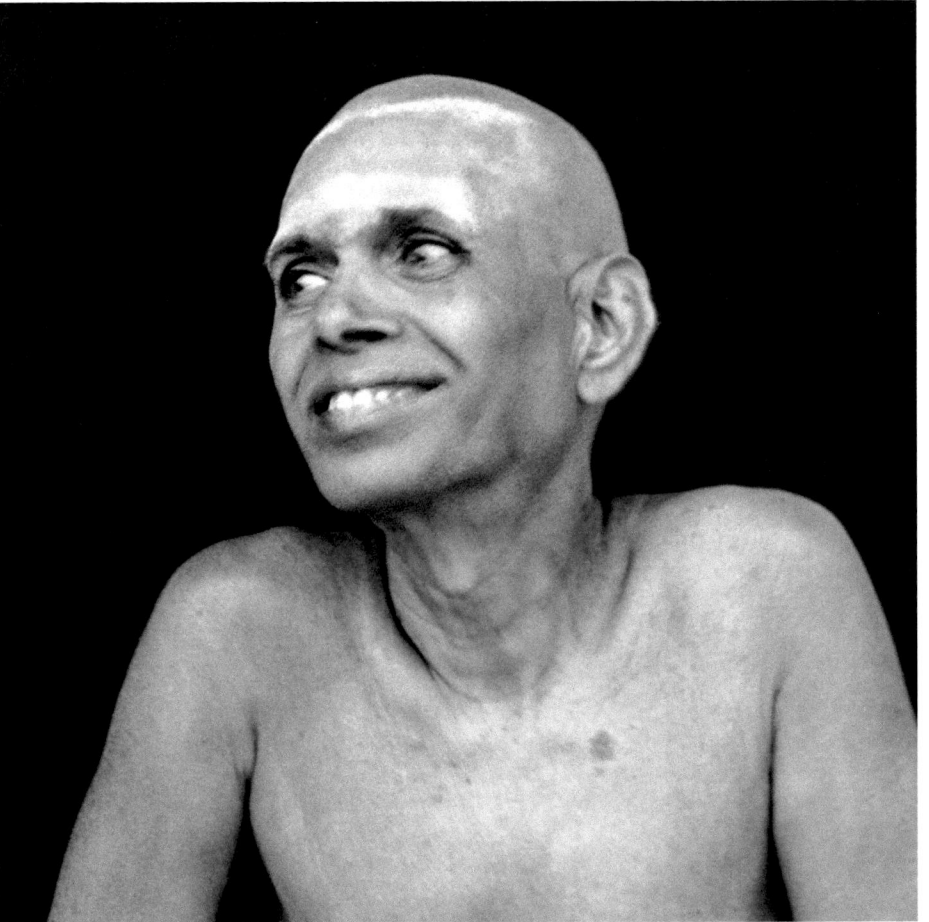

# Nan Yar

## Who Am I?

All living beings desire to be happy always, without any misery. In everyone there is observed supreme love for oneself. And happiness alone is the cause of love. In order therefore, to gain that happiness which is one's nature and which is experienced in the state of deep sleep, where there is no mind, one should know oneself. To achieve this, the Path of Knowledge, the inquiry in the form of 'Who am I?', is the principal means.

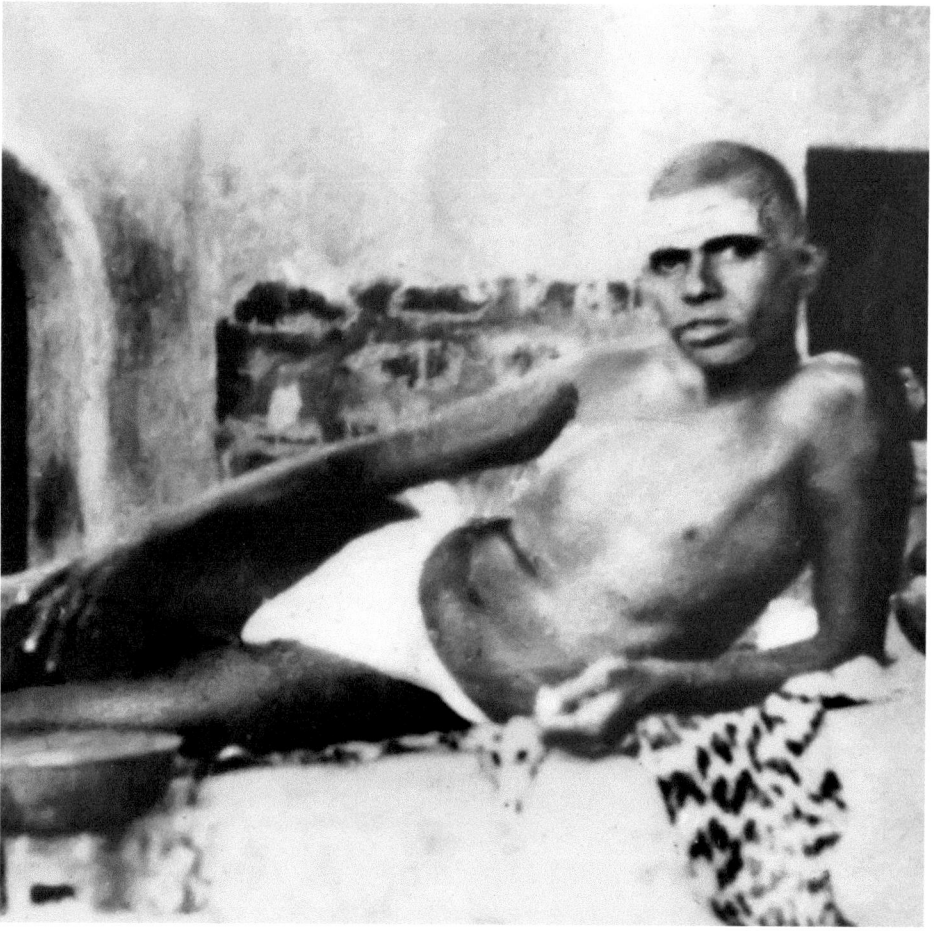

# 1. Who am I?

The gross [*physical*] body which is composed of the seven humours (*dhatus*) [*body tissues*], I am not; the five cognitive sense organs, such as the senses of hearing, touch, sight, taste and smell, which apprehend their respective objects, namely sound, touch, colour, taste and odour, I am not; the five cognitive sense organs, such as the organs of speech, locomotion, grasping, excreting and enjoying, I am not; the five vital airs, such as *prana* [*life force*], which perform respectively the five functions of in-breathing, I am not; even the mind which thinks, I am not; the nescience [*ignorance*] too, which is endowed only with the residual impressions of objects and in which there are no objects and no functions, I am not.

[*I am not the physical body, nor the five senses, nor the thinking mind. I am not the unconscious mind containing the tendencies of mind, which remain even in deep sleep.*]

You are really the infinite,
pure Being, the Self Absolute.
You are always that Self
and nothing but that Self.

## 2. If I am none of these, then who am I?

After negating all of the above mentioned as 'not this', 'not this', this Awareness which alone remains – that I am.

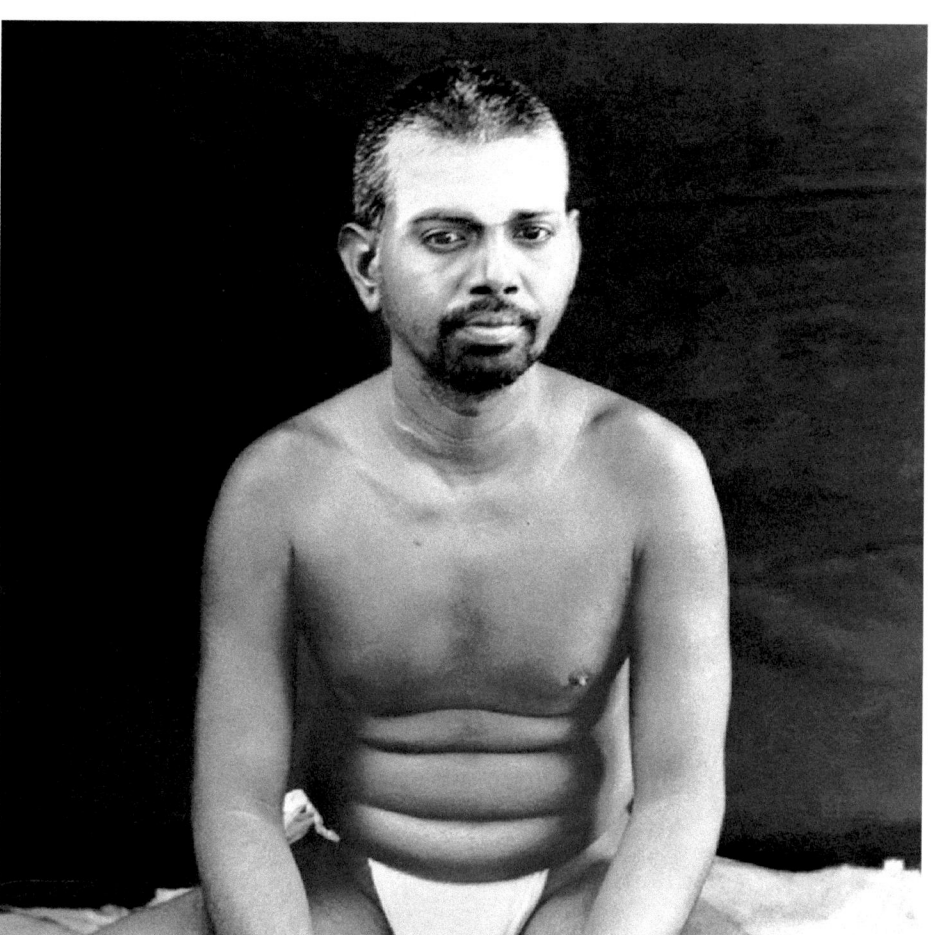

### 3. What is the nature of Awareness?

The nature of Awareness is Existence [*Being*] - Consciousness - Bliss.

## 4. When will the realisation of the Self be gained?

When the world which is what-is-seen has been removed, there will be realisation of the Self which is the Seer.

[*When the perception of the world is not taken as real, there will be realisation of the Self, which is the one who sees.*]

The *jnani*\* is fully aware
that the true state of Being remains fixed
and that all actions go on around him.
His nature does not change,
he looks on everything with unconcern
and remains blissful himself.

**5. Will there not be realisation of the Self even while the world is there (taken as real)?**

There will not be.

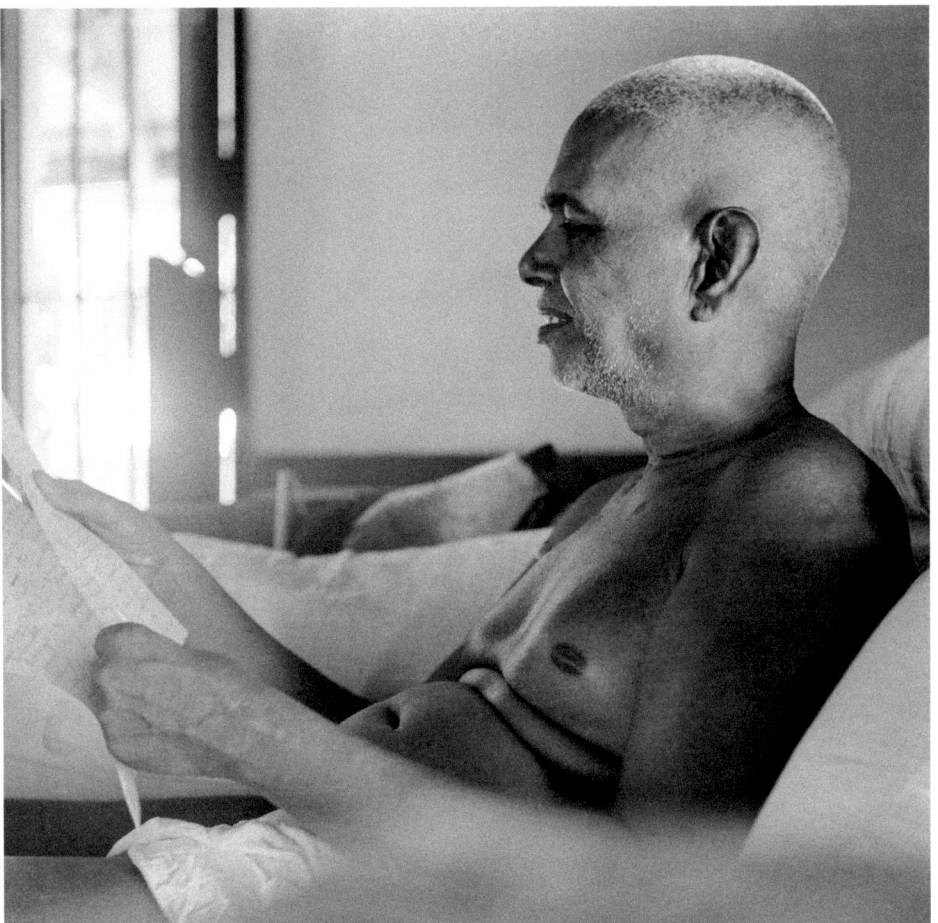

## 6. Why?

The seer and the object seen are like the rope and the snake. Just as the knowledge of the rope which is the substratum [*essence*] will not arise unless the false knowledge of the illusory serpent goes, so the realisation of the Self which is the substratum will not be gained unless the belief that the world is real is removed.

## 7. When will the world which is the object seen be removed?

When the mind, which is the cause of all cognition [*knowledge*] and of all actions, becomes quiescent [*still*], the world will disappear.

If we set aside all thoughts and see,
there will be no such thing
as mind remaining separate.
Other than thoughts,
there is no such thing as the world.

## 8. What is the nature of the mind?

What is called 'mind' is a wondrous power residing in the Self. It causes all thoughts to arise. Apart from thoughts, there is no such thing as mind. Therefore, thought is the nature of mind. Apart from thoughts, there is no independent entity called the world. In deep sleep there are no thoughts, and there is no world. In the states of waking and dream, there are thoughts, and there is a world also. Just as the spider emits the thread (of the web) out of itself and again withdraws it into itself, likewise the mind projects the world out of itself and again resolves it into itself.

[*continued over page*]

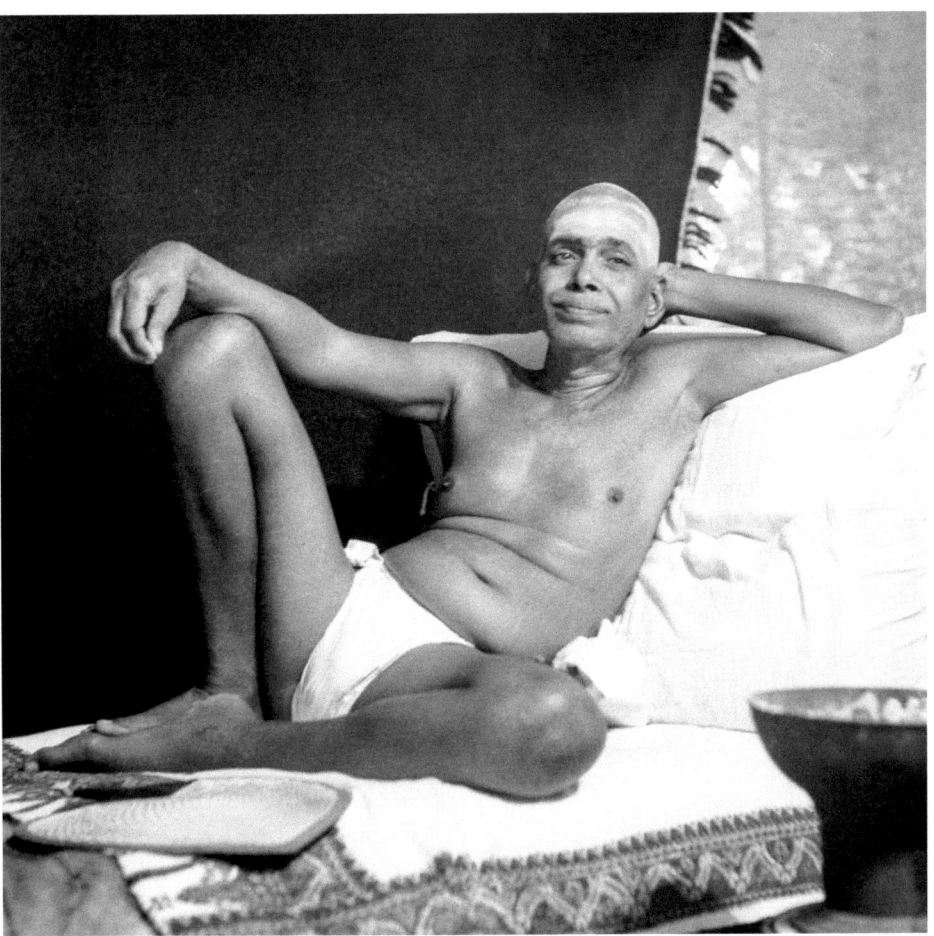

*[Question 8 continued]*

When the mind comes out of the Self, the world appears. Therefore, when the world appears (to be real), the Self does not appear; and when the Self appears (shines) the world does not appear [*is not taken as real*]. When one persistently inquires into the nature of the mind, the mind will end leaving the Self (as the residue). What is referred to as the Self is the *Atman**. The mind always exists only in dependence on something gross [*physical*]; it cannot stay alone. It is the mind [*ego*] that is called the subtle body or the soul (*jiva**).

## 9. What is the path of inquiry for understanding the nature of the mind?

That which rises as 'I' in this body is the mind. If one inquires as to where in the body the thought 'I' rises first, one would discover that it rises in the Heart [hridayam*, *spiritual heart*]. That is the place of the mind's origin. Even if one thinks constantly 'I-I', one will be led to that place. Of all the thoughts that arise in the mind, the 'I'-thought is the first. It is only after the rise of this that the other thoughts arise. It is after the appearance of the first personal pronoun [*I*] that the second and the third personal pronouns [*you, he, she and they*] appear; without the first personal pronoun there will not be the second and the third.

Just drop all seeking,
turn your attention inward,
and sacrifice your mind
to the One Self radiating
in the Heart of your very being.

## 10. How will the mind become quiescent [*still*]?

By the inquiry 'Who am I?'. The thought 'Who am I?' will destroy all other thoughts, and like the stick used for stirring the burning pyre [*funeral fire*], it will itself in the end get destroyed. Then, there will arise Self-realisation.

## 11. What is the means for constantly holding on to the thought 'Who am I?'

When other thoughts arise, one should not pursue them, but should inquire: 'To whom do they arise?' It does not matter how many thoughts arise. As each thought arises, one should inquire with diligence [*constant effort*], 'To whom has this thought arisen?'. The answer that would emerge would be 'to me'. Thereupon if one inquires 'Who am I?', the mind will go back to its source; and the thought that arose will become quiescent [*still*]. With repeated practice in this manner, the mind will develop the skill to stay in its source.

When the mind that is subtle goes out through the brain and the sense-organs, the gross [*physical*] names and forms appear; when it stays in the Heart, the names and forms disappear.

[*continued over page*]

*[Question 11 continued]*

Not letting the mind go out, but retaining it in the Heart is what is called 'inwardness' (*antarmukha*). Letting the mind go out of the Heart is known as 'externalisation' (*bahirmukha*).

When the mind stays in the Heart, the 'I' which is the source of all thoughts will go, and the Self which ever exists will shine. Whatever one does, one should do without the egoity 'I'. If one acts in that way, all will appear as of the nature of *Shiva*\* (God).

Find out to whom are the thoughts.
Where from do they arise?
They must spring up
from the conscious Self.
Thereafter the realisation
of the one Infinite Existence
becomes possible.

## 12. Are there no other means for making the mind quiescent [*still*]?

Other than inquiry, there are no adequate means. If through other means it is sought to control the mind, the mind will appear to be controlled, but will again go forth [*arise*]. Through the control of breath also, the mind will become quiescent; but it will be quiescent only so long as the breath remains controlled, and when the breath resumes the mind also will again start moving and will wander as impelled [*driven*] by residual impressions [*thoughts*]. The source is the same for both mind and breath. Thought, indeed, is the nature of the mind.

The thought 'I' is the first thought of the mind; and that is egoity. It is from that whence egoity originates that breath also originates. Therefore, when the mind becomes quiescent, the breath is controlled, and when the breath is controlled the mind becomes quiescent. But in deep sleep, although the mind becomes quiescent, the breath does not stop.

[*continued over page*]

*[Question 12 continued]*

This is because of the will of God, so that the body may be preserved and other people may not be under the impression that it is dead. In the state of waking and in *samadhi**  [*glimpse of the Self*], when the mind becomes quiescent the breath is controlled. Breath is the gross [*physical*] form of the mind. Till the time of death, the mind keeps breath in the body; and when the body dies, the mind takes the breath along with it. Therefore, the exercise of breath control is only an aid for rendering the mind quiescent (*manonigraha*); it will not destroy the mind (*manonasa**).

Like the practice of breath control, meditation on the forms of God, repetition of *mantras** [*sacred sounds*], restriction on food, are but aids for rendering the mind quiescent.

*[continued over page]*

[*Question 12 continued*]

Through meditation on the forms of God and through repetition of *mantras*, the mind becomes one-pointed. The mind will always be wandering. Just as when a chain is given to an elephant to hold in its trunk it will go along grasping the chain and nothing else, so also when the mind is occupied with a name or form it will grasp that alone.

When the mind expands in the form of countless thoughts, each thought becomes weak; but as thoughts get resolved the mind becomes one-pointed and strong; for such a mind Self-inquiry will become easy. Of all the restrictive rules, that relating to the taking of *sattvic*\* [*pure*] food in moderate quantities is the best; by observing this rule, the *sattvic* quality of mind will increase, and that will be helpful to Self-inquiry.

Self-inquiry directly leads to
Self-realisation by removing
the obstacles, which make you think
that the Self is not already realised.

**13. The residual impressions (thoughts) of objects appear unending like the waves of an ocean. When will all of them get destroyed?**

As the meditation on the Self rises higher and higher, the thoughts will get destroyed.

## 14. Is it possible for the residual impressions of objects that come from beginningless time, as it were, to be resolved, and for one to remain as the pure Self?

Without yielding to the doubt 'Is it possible, or not?', one should persistently hold on to the meditation on the Self. Even if one be a great sinner, one should not worry and weep 'O! I am a sinner, how can I be saved? One should completely renounce the thought 'I am a sinner' and concentrate keenly on meditation on the Self alone; then, one would surely succeed.

There are not two minds – one good and the other evil; the mind is only one. It is the residual impressions [*thoughts*] that are of two kinds – auspicious and inauspicious. When the mind is under the influence of auspicious impressions it is called good; and when it is under the influence of inauspicious impressions it is regarded as evil.

[*continued over page*]

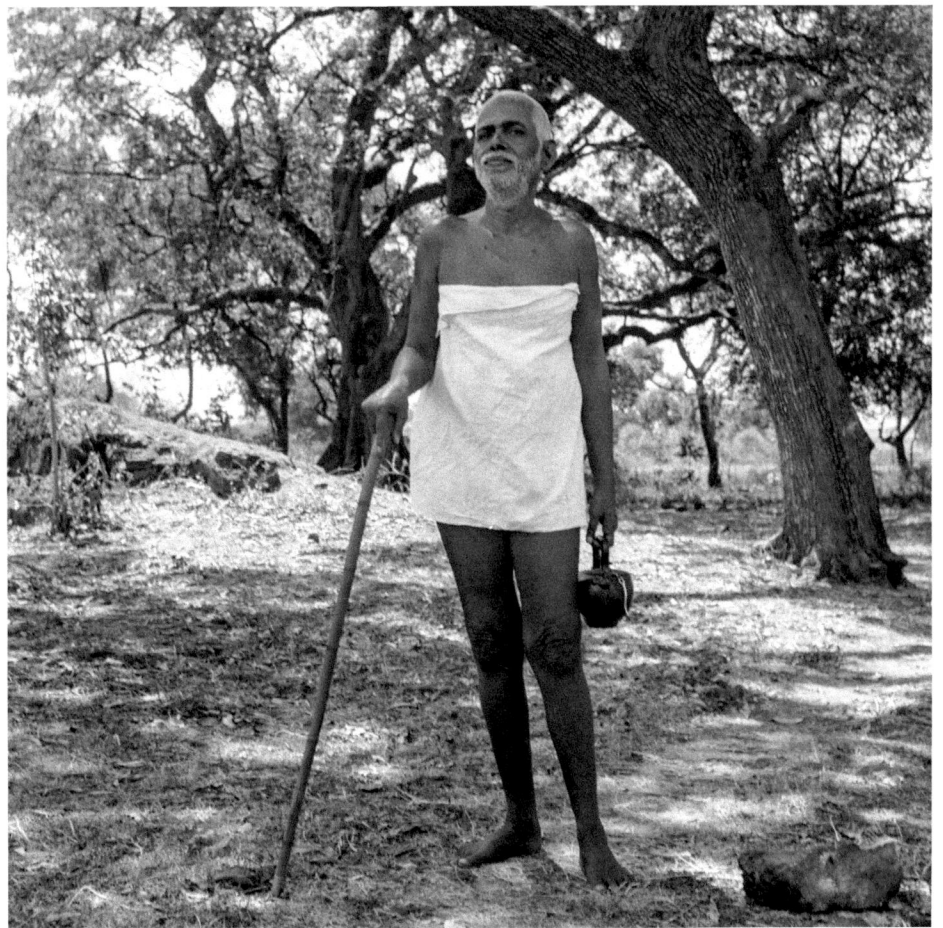

*[Question 14 continued]*

The mind should not be allowed to wander towards worldly objects and what concerns other people. However bad other people may be, one should bear no hatred for them. Both desire and hatred should be eschewed [*avoided*].

All that one gives to others one gives to one's self. If this truth is understood who will not give to others? When one's self arises all arises; when one's self becomes quiescent [*still*] all becomes quiescent. To the extent we behave with humility, to that extent there will result good. If the mind is rendered quiescent, one may live anywhere.

There is a state when
words cease and silence prevails.
Silence is the ocean
into which all the rivers
of all religions discharge themselves.
It is the speech of the Self.
That which Is, is Silence.

## 15. How long should inquiry be practised?

As long as there are impressions of objects in the mind, so long the inquiry 'Who am I?' is required. As thoughts arise they should be destroyed then and there in the very place of their origin, through inquiry. If one resorts to contemplation of the Self unintermittently [*constantly*], until the Self is gained, that alone would do. As long as there are enemies within the fortress, they will continue to sally forth [*come out*]; if they are destroyed as they emerge, the fortress will fall into our hands.

## 16. What is the nature of the Self?

What exists in truth is the Self alone. The world, the individual soul and God are appearances in it, like silver in mother-of-pearl; these three appear at the same time and disappear at the same time. The Self is that where there is absolutely no 'I'-thought. That is called 'Silence'. The Self itself is the world; the Self itself is 'I'; the Self itself is God; all is *Shiva*, the Self.

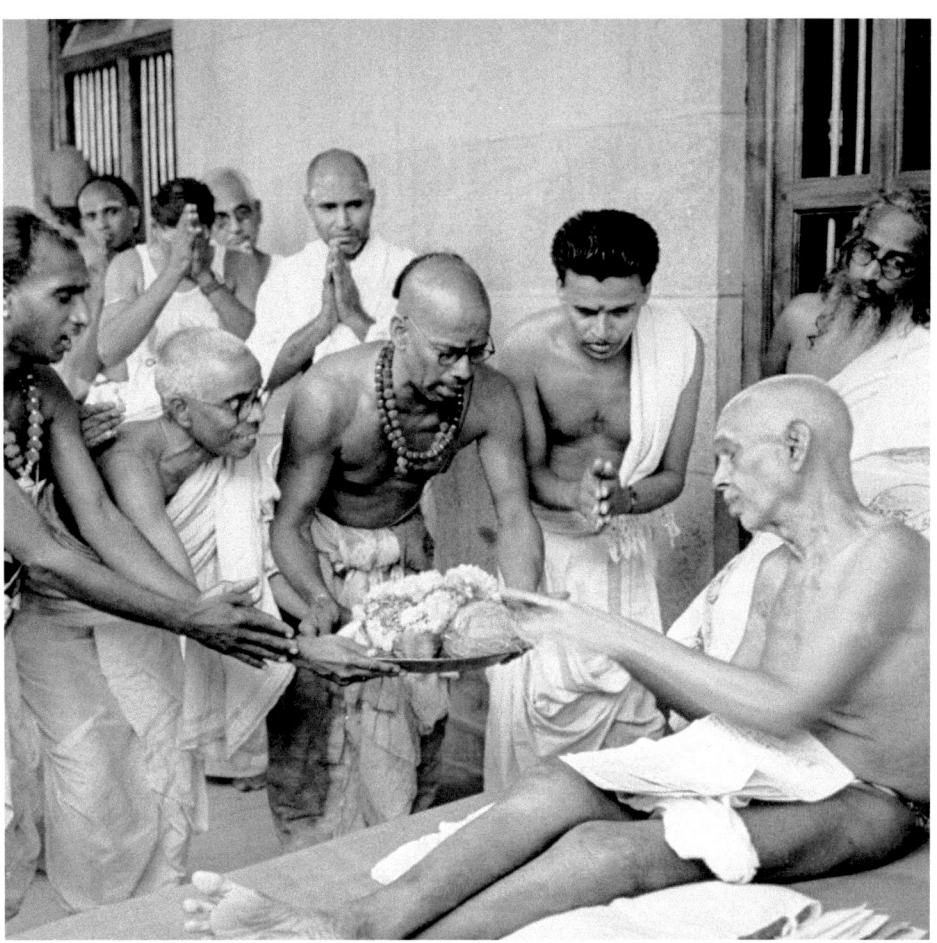

## 17. Is not everything the work of God?

Without desire, resolve, or effort, the sun rises; and in its mere presence, the sun-stone emits fire, the lotus blooms, water evaporates, people perform their various functions and then rest. Just as in the presence of the magnet the needle moves, it is by virtue of the mere presence of God that the souls governed by the three (cosmic) functions [*creation, sustaining life and dissolution*] or the fivefold divine activity [Vedantic *theory of creation*] perform their actions and then rest, in accordance with their respective *karmas*\* [*cosmic law*].

God has no resolve [*intention*]; no *karma* attaches itself to Him. That is like worldly actions not affecting the sun, or like the merits and demerits [*good and bad qualities*] of the other four elements not affecting all-pervading space.

God or *Guru*\* never forsakes
the devotee who surrenders.
God takes the form of a *Guru*
and appears to the devotee,
teaches him the Truth,
and purifies his mind by association.

## 18. Of the devotees, who is the greatest?

He who gives himself up to the Self that is God is the most excellent devotee. Giving one's self up to God means remaining constantly in the Self without giving room for the rise of any thoughts other than that of the Self.

    Whatever burdens are thrown on God, He bears them. Since the supreme power of God makes all things move, why should we, without submitting ourselves to it, constantly worry ourselves with thoughts as to what should be done and how, and what should not be done and how not? We know that the train carries all loads, so after getting on it why should we carry our small luggage on our head to our discomfort, instead of putting it down in the train and feeling at ease?

## 19. What is non-attachment?

As thoughts arise, destroying them utterly without any residue in the very place of their origin is non-attachment. Just as the pearl-diver ties a stone to his waist, sinks to the bottom of the sea and there takes the pearls, so each one of us should be endowed with non-attachment, dive within oneself and obtain the Self-Pearl.

## 20. Is it possible for God and the *Guru* to effect the liberation of a soul?

God and the *Guru* will only show the way to liberation; they will not by themselves take the soul to the state of liberation. In truth, God and the *Guru* are not different.

Just as the prey which has fallen into the jaws of a tiger has no escape, so those who have come within the ambit [*presence*] of the *Guru's* gracious look will be saved by the *Guru* and will not get lost; yet, each one should, by his own effort pursue the path shown by God or *Guru* and gain liberation.

One can know oneself only with one's own eye of knowledge, and not with somebody else's. Does he who is Rama require the help of a mirror to know that he is Rama?

You are awareness.
Awareness is another name for you.
Since you are awareness
there is no need to attain
or cultivate it.

**21. Is it necessary for one who longs for liberation to inquire into the nature of categories (*tattvas*) [Vedantic *system categorising existence*]?**

Just as one who wants to throw away garbage has no need to analyse it and see what it is, so one who wants to know the Self has no need to count the number of categories or inquire into their characteristics; what he has to do is to reject altogether the categories that hide the Self. The world should be considered like a dream.

## 22. Is there no difference between waking and dream?

Waking is long and dream short; other than this there is no difference. Just as waking happenings seem real while awake, so do those in a dream while dreaming. In dream the mind takes on another body. In both waking and dream states thoughts, names and forms occur simultaneously.

## 23. Is it any use reading books for those who long for liberation?

All the texts say that in order to gain liberation one should render the mind quiescent [*still*]; therefore their conclusive teaching is that the mind should be rendered quiescent; once this has been understood there is no need for endless reading.

In order to quieten the mind one has only to inquire within oneself what one's Self is; how could this search be done in books? One should know one's Self with one's own eye of wisdom. The Self is within the five sheaths [*body, breath, mind, intellect, ignorance*]; but books are outside them. Since the Self has to be inquired into by discarding the five sheaths, it is futile to search for it in books. There will come a time when one will have to forget all that one has learned.

The seat of realisation is within
and the seeker cannot find it
as an object outside him.
That seat is bliss and is
the core of all beings.

## 24. What is happiness?

Happiness is the very nature of the Self; happiness and the Self are not different. There is no happiness in any object of the world. We imagine through our ignorance that we derive happiness from objects. When the mind goes out, it experiences misery. In truth, when its desires are fulfilled, it returns to its own place and enjoys the happiness that is the Self. Similarly, in the states of sleep, *samadhi* and fainting, and when the object desired is obtained or the object disliked is removed, the mind becomes inward-turned, and enjoys pure Self-Happiness.

Thus the mind moves without rest alternately going out of the Self and returning to it. Under the tree the shade is pleasant; out in the open the heat is scorching. A person who has been going about in the sun feels cool when he reaches the shade. Someone who keeps on going from the shade into the sun and then back into the shade is a fool. A wise man stays permanently in the shade.

[*continued over page*]

[*Question 24 continued*]

Similarly, the mind of the one who knows the truth does not leave *Brahman*\* [*absolute reality*]. The mind of the ignorant, on the contrary, revolves in the world, feeling miserable, and for a little time returns to *Brahman* to experience happiness. In fact, what is called the world is only thought. When the world disappears, i.e., when there is no thought, the mind experiences happiness; and when the world appears, it goes through misery.

## 25. What is wisdom-insight (*jnana drishti*)?

Remaining quiet is what is called wisdom-insight. To remain quiet is to resolve the mind in the Self. Telepathy, knowing past, present and future happenings and clairvoyance do not constitute wisdom-insight.

'No desire' is the greatest bliss.
It can be realised only by experience.
Even an emperor is no match
for a man with no desire.

## 26. What is the relation between desirelessness and wisdom?

Desirelessness is wisdom. The two are not different; they are the same. Desirelessness is refraining from turning the mind towards any objects. Wisdom means the appearance of no object. In other words, not seeking what is other than the Self is detachment or desirelessness; not leaving the Self is wisdom.

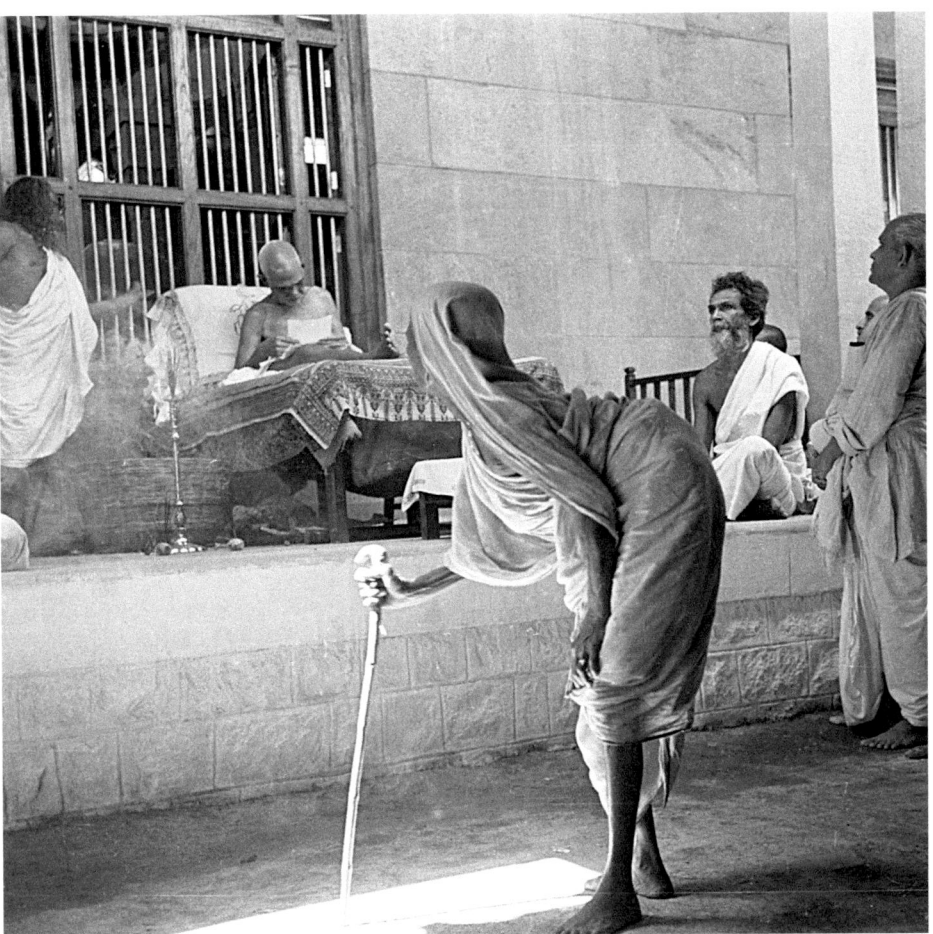

## 27. What is the difference between inquiry and meditation?

Inquiry consists in retaining [*keeping*] the mind in the Self. Meditation consists in thinking that one's self is *Brahman*, Existence [*Being*]-Consciousness-Bliss.

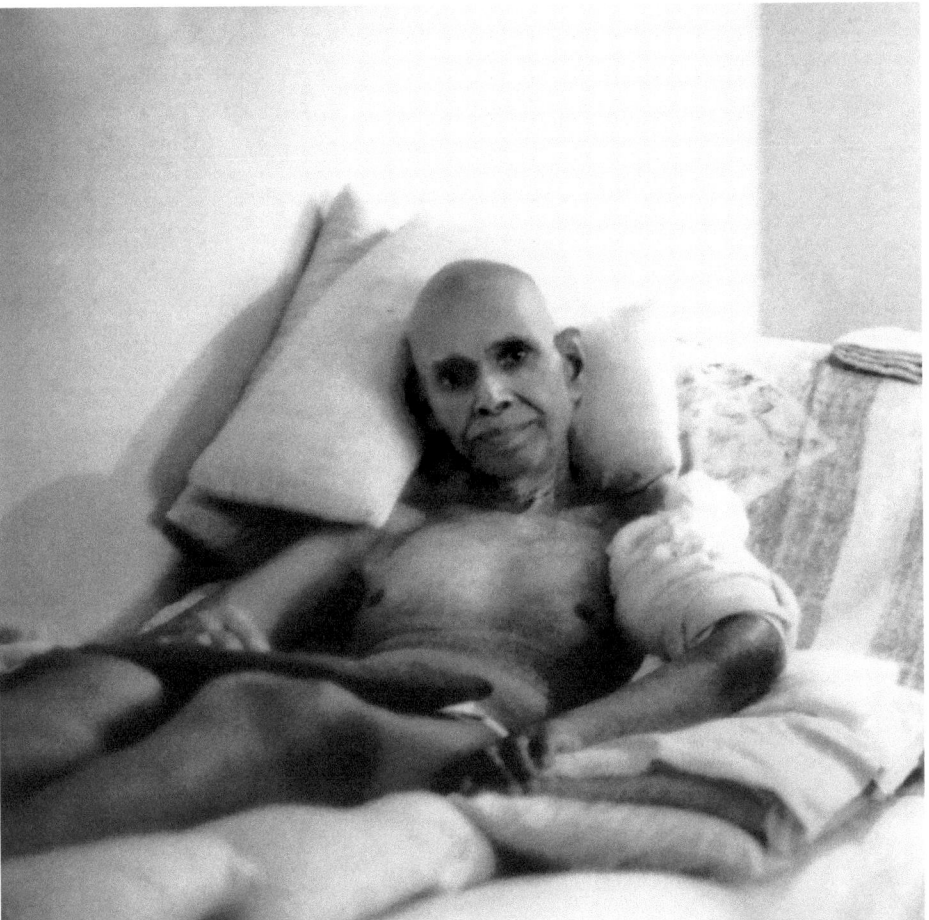

## 28. What is liberation?

Inquiring into the nature of one's self that is in bondage, and realising one's true nature is liberation.

# Glossary

**Atman**  The inmost Self or Spirit of man.

**Brahman**  The impersonal, absolute reality – the Self.

**Guru**  Literally: the one who removes ignorance. A teacher in the religious or spiritual sense, commonly used in Hinduism and Buddhism. The importance of finding a true *Guru* is given as a prerequisite for attaining Self-realisation.

**hridayam**  Literally, 'this is the centre'. Usually translated as 'Heart' or 'Spiritual Heart'. In Ramana Maharshi's words: 'Heart means the very core of one's being, the Self, without which there is nothing whatever.'

**jiva**  The individual soul, which, until liberation, will continue to incarnate. In essence, it is one with the Universal Soul.

**jnani**  One who has realised the Self. One who has attained realisation by the path of knowledge, meaning the knowledge of what is real and what is not real.

**karma**  Cosmic law of cause and effect, the result of an individual's past actions, which is said to invariably return to him at some point in time. Also: the collective storehouse of merit or demerit from all of an individual's past actions.

**manonasa**  Literally: extinction of the mind. It particularly means destruction of the thinking mind as the practical mind is needed for daily functioning.

| | |
|---|---|
| **mantra** | Sacred sound. In the Hindu traditions a sound from the *Vedas*. Repeated either orally or mentally and used as an aid in bringing concentration to the mind. The most well-known *mantra* is the original sound OM. |
| **nirvana** | Blowing out, such as a flame. Annihilation of desire, passion and ego; liberation, characterised by freedom and bliss. |
| **samadhi** | Direct but temporary experience of the Self. The experiencing subject becomes one with the experienced object, the mind becomes still. |
| **samsara** | The continuous cycle of birth and death caused by illusion and desire. |
| **sattvic** | Pure, of the nature of *Sat* (Truth). Also used in the context of a diet supporting Self-realisation. |

**Self**  The term most commonly used in translation for *Atman*; the unchanging awareness, consciousness itself.

**Shankara**  *Adi Shankara*: Indian sage of the 9th century who is considered the most influential figure of *Advaita Vedanta*.

**Shiva**  Another name for God, or Truth. In Hindu mythology, *Shiva* (the destroyer), *Brahma* (the creator) and *Vishnu* (the preserver), are 3 of the main deities.

**Vedanta**  A metaphysical philosophy derived from the *Upanishads*, the concluding portion of the *Vedas* consisting of 108 verses. The *Upanishads* are the texts from which all *Vedanta* philosophy is derived.

# RAMANA BOOKS SELECTION
## A Choice of Titles on Sri Ramana

### Be As You Are – The Teachings of Sri Ramana Maharshi
edited by David Godman, Penguin Books, Tiruvannamalai, 1985

### The Collected Works of Ramana Maharshi
Sri Ramanasramam, Tiruvannamalai, 6th revised edition, 1996

### Day by Day with Bhagavan
from the Diary of A. Devaraja Mudaliar, Sri Ramanasramam, Tiruvannamalai, 2002

### Garland of Guru's Sayings (Guru Vachaka Kovai)
Murugunar, translated by Swaminathan, Sri Ramanasrama, Tiruvannamalai, 1990

### Guru Ramana
S.S. Cohen, Sri Ramanasramam Tiruvannamalai, 1974 edition

### Self-Inquiry (Vicharasangraham) of Sri Ramana Maharshi
translated by Dr T.M.P. Mahadevan, Sri Ramanasramam, Tiruvannamalai, 1994

### Talks with Sri Ramana Maharshi
compiled by Sri Munagala Venkataramiah, Sri Ramanasramam, Tiruvannamalai, 1st edition, 1955

### The Last Days and Maha Nirvana of Bhagavan Sri Ramana
Viswanatha Swami, Arthur Osborne and T.N. Krishnaswamy, Sri Ramanasrama, Tiruvannamalai, 1997

## Ramanasramam Bookshop
Tiruvannamalai, South India
bookstall@sriramanamaharshi.org
**www.bookstore.sriramanamaharshi.org**

# OPEN SKY PRESS
Publishers of Fine Quality Spiritual Books

**Aham Sphurana - A Glimpse of Self Realisation** offers fascinating dialogues and stories of Sri Ramana Maharshi recorded by Sri Gajapathi Aiyyer in the summer 1936, at Ramana Ashram. This book contains a selection from the complete manuscript Aham Sphurana. This selection, a brilliant treasure, speaks for itself. Beside the detailed teachings on Self-Enquiry, Surrender and Jnana, it exposes a new glimpse of Bhagavan's personal day-to-day life at fifty-six, in his middle age.

**Arunachala Shiva** paints an intimate picture of Sri Ramana Maharshi's life, clearly laying out the core of his teaching. Included in this book are in-depth, fascinating commentaries from experts on Sri Ramana. With hundred beautiful photos of Bhagavan, the ashram, and Arunachala. In addition, the full length film shows the best of the interviews, together with lovely footage of Sri Ramana, his ashram and Arunachala.

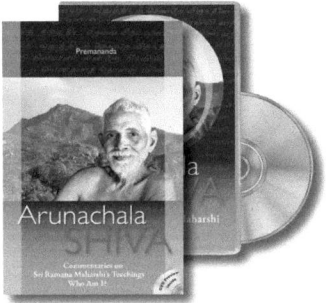

## Open Sky Press
Tel +49 (0)2173 203 9595
office@openskypress.com
**www.openskypress.com**